Golf is similar
to the game we call life.

You get bad breaks from good shots.

You get good breaks from bad shots.

But you have to play the ball where it lies.

BOBBY JONES

WORD FROM THE AUTHOR

There are many reasons I am drawn to the game of golf. It is a great connector with people. It's a game you can continue to play and actually improve on as you age. It's a great escape into the outdoors. It's challenging and stimulating. It's challenging and stimulating. Did I mention it's challenging and stimulating?

Unlike many of my friends I now play with, I started playing the game later in life. I was in my late fifties when I first took the game seriously. One of the most motivating factors in picking up the game was the opportunity to create an enjoyable way to spend time with my son. He started the game as a youngster taking lessons and attending golf camps during his summer vacations. It has been a great way for us to spend time together.

Another motivating factor connecting me to the game is the annual golf tournament held as the major fundraiser for the nonprofit which I head. Our organization, *Banded Brothers*, has raised over a quarter million dollars since our creation by organizing golfers each year on the first Monday in October to help those less fortunate.

The game of golf has been a blessing for me in these ways and many others. Some of my most enjoyable moments with my best friends and family have been centered around the game.

I hope you enjoy this book regardless whether you enjoy chasing the little white ball. I hope my scribble touches you in a way that makes your day brighter.

I am neither a professional author nor an expert in grammar. I hope in some way that fact makes your reading a little more fun and adventurous. I do enjoy the connection with people and sharing experiences that enrich our relationships.

Charlie

DEDICATION OF THIS BOOK

I dedicate this book to my friend John Thomas Kelly aka "Coach". The content of this book is based on two closely held things in my life that I enjoy and define me. The first is my faith. As a follower of Jesus, I have tried to live my life in a way that would be pleasing to God. I fail miserably at that on a daily basis but as a worldly human made of the flesh, I have to accept that. But every day I rise and try to do better. The second theme of this book is golf.

Coach Kelly has been at the forefront of both of these life passions. Our friendship was founded years ago in the formation of our nonprofit *Banded Brothers*. Coach was one of the first financial supporters and charter members continuing in that role to this day. His love and commitment to the cause of our organization has been a major key to its success. As of the date of this publication, our organization has raised over a quarter million dollars of which we have doled out in hundreds of small gifts to people in our local community who found themselves wedged in the cracks of traditional assistance channels.

Coach has been the backbone of our main fundraiser that has allowed *Banded Brothers* to recognize our past accomplishments. That fundraiser has been our annual golf tournament. Coach has used his contacts and network of friends to recruit the teams, hole sponsors and donations that have made this event a huge success.

Prior to becoming the friends we are today, Coach would approach me on Sundays at church and slip a check into my pocket without saying a word. Enjoying a successful career in the insurance industry, he was quick to give and bless others from the bounty of blessing he had received in his life.

Before his insurance career, Coach spent his early adult life as a school teacher and coach. Past students, players and business clients are quick to pay this man the many accolades he so deserves. There are few in our community who don't love and appreciate this man. There are few who have not been touched by his generosity in some capacity.

Coach has left his mark and made a difference in the lives of so many. I am blessed to say that I am one.

WE LOVE YOU
COACH KELLY

GOOD PUTT

Regardless of the long held assumption that a day on the golf course is just a bunch of testosterone filled men telling lies and dirty jokes while they chase a little white ball, I can attest to the contrary. From my experience, most men are considerate of the performance of fellow players. For example, you rarely hear one golfer suggest to another that they just hit a crappy shot. When bad shots are fired, you can expect more silence in lieu of criticism.

Recently I faced about a thirty foot putt. After surveying the fall of the green and adjusting accordingly, I struck the ball with the force I estimated to be appropriate to reach the cup. My ball fell just inches from the hole. One fellow player simply commented "good putt". I have heard those words of assurance many times before. After hearing the comment, another member of our group shouted in protest: "the only good putt is the one that goes in the hole" he exclaimed.

On some degree, I can't really disagree with his assessment. The object is to sink the putt. Anything short of that is second place. However consider these statistics on how PGA Tour Pros perform on first try puts. 5 feet: 65% are made. 10 feet: 15 to 30% are made. 20 feet: 16% are made. 30 feet: 9% are made. 40 feet: only 6% are made. An ole pro I know offers great advice on putting saying: "if you want to putt better, hit the ball closer to the hole".

Putting is a lot similar to life. It can often be difficult and requires considerable practice to overcome its challenges. As in putting, it's important in life to recognize and consider the environment (lie) and human conditions (green) before you speak or act (strike the ball). As reflected in the aforementioned statistics first time strikes, many more times than not, miss the target.

Whenever our family and friends miss the targets in life, it's important that we offer the encouraging words: "nice putt". Criticism and degrading comments only add to their frustration and are not consistent with the love that God expects each of us to have for each other.

KENT

Played in a golf tournament on Thursday. The teams were comprised of high school coaches from across the state along with invited boosters. My son and I played with my cousin Eddie who is the men's basketball coach at Garner High School along with his assistant coach Kent Bloms. I have written about Eddie in the past of the love and admiration I have for him. I always enjoy being with him. Believe me, it is very high energy with never a dull moment. We were served a spread lunch of bar-be-que, chicken, and shrimp catered by Clyde Coopers. We teed off at two and had a great day shooting a best ball score of 62.

My story begins when Kent showed up carrying his clubs. Now .... I tell you with absolutely zero exaggeration, that his clubs were the oldest, most worn and ragged set I had never laid eyes on. These clubs would not have brought fifty cents at a yard sale. The cloth bag was torn and ripped with the bottom pocket very much akin to a rat's nest. There were two woods (that were actually made of wood) a couple of rusted irons and a putter that looked like a pipe wrench. All comments on the clubs were withheld until Eddie unleashed a demeaning tirade of insulting and degrading commentary. Remember we all are friends.

I got to admit I had some serious reservations about Kent's performance considering his clubs. This young man was a horse easily towering over six feet and built like an anvil. Eddie, Joseph and I had each hit our ball off the first tee. Our shots flew long and straight all landing in positions for a nice approach shot to the green. I stood eagerly awaiting Kent's shot. He stepped up to the tee with the most awful looking club and ripped it straight down the fairway thirty yards past our previous shots. All concern in regards to inadequate equipment immediately evaporated. Kent continued to play well the entire day driving, pitching and putting with less than adequate equipment to say the least.

We all know stories of the underdog type. The best looking car does not always win the race. On the other side of the coin Steve Ballmer, the world's richest professional sports team owner, can't win a championship.

As followers of Jesus, we find our hope knowing that God does not "call the equipped but equips the called". There is no substitute for hope, drive and determination in facing the challenges of life. We all occasionally find ourselves sulking in the pity of life's unfairness. Fact is life is not unfair. Life is what we make it. You can shoot a respectable round of golf with a lousy set of clubs. Thanks Kent for the lesson.

TRAVIS

If you are a follower of Jesus, allow me to take the liberty of assuming that "prayer" is a foundational piece of your relationship with God. We are told in 1 Thessalonians 5:17 to "pray without ceasing." While it's logical to recognize that we cannot spend all our life on our knees, let me suggest that we can have a prayerful attitude at all times. This attitude is spawned and further cultivated in our faith and the acknowledgment of our dependence on the Father as we travel this journey of life.

I was working in my yard on Saturday re-seeding all the grass I had seeded the week before that was washed away by all the recent rain. My buddy, Travis, was alongside me as he is every Saturday assisting me in whatever project is at hand. Travis is one of the most spirit filled and thankful people I know. This fact is even more impressive when you consider his life situation. He has no permanent job because he is a single parent with two kids and can't afford childcare. He works odd jobs and simply does the best he can.

The birth mother of his children subscribes to many addictions and squanders the public assistance she gets on things other than the children. Until recently, Travis' main mode of transportation was walking and a worn out bicycle. It is not uncommon for Travis to walk 10 miles for a $15.00 grass mowing gig. Several years ago Travis was struck on his bicycle sustaining injuries that later required brain surgery. My point here is to establish Travis as a man facing many challenges.

Now .... let's get back to "prayer" and "grass". As Travis and I worked aerating the soil and casting grass seeds, I found myself praying to God that the grass would grow. I meditated deeply whispering payers to God that He would hold back the torrential rains and provide just enough for the newly sown seeds to prosper. I continued in this spiritual trance for some time as I busily went about the task at hand until I noticed Travis joyously working away.

It was then that I imagined all the prayers that might be going on inside his heart. Will the utilities be disconnected? Will the children remain healthy considering he has no insurance? Will there be work next week? Will there be gas for the lawn mower if I get a grass cutting job? Will my landlord work with me on my past due rent or will my family be homeless? An overwhelming feeling of guilt and shame came over me realizing I was praying for something as menial as grass. Maybe you get my point.

Tomorrow Banded Brothers will hold our 10th annual golf tournament to raise funds for people like Travis. There are so many among us. There are a multitude of brothers and sisters with needs far greater than our own. As for "prayer" ...... please pray for our golf event and for Travis. Hope it's a great day. Travis plans to join us.

WEEDS

There are three golf courses within a five mile radius of my home. No !!! wait a minute, there are just two .... one closed several weeks back. Yes, I said closed. It seems the real estate developer who owned the property felt a financial necessity to close the links and build more houses. Could he really do this you say ??? Well yes .... his right to do so was written into the neighborhood covenants and all homeowner purchase agreements. Remember all those AGREE TO TERMS blocks you check without reading the fine print? Can this kinda thing really happen ?? Just ask the residents of Crooked Creek. I ain't seen no creek but the whole deal sounds crooked to me.

I pass the property every day on my way to work. Hole numbers one, eight and ten tee boxes along with number seven fairway can be seen in full view from the highway. The reality of the course's closing presents itself in complete and full view as the once manicured landscape has been transformed to now a weed infested wasteland. It's like a black eye for the community. Many are affected. This is the place where my son attended annual golf camps and played many high school team matches. It was a safe haven hangout for him and his golf buddies where he traded washing carts for free golf. The community has lost much more than a golf course. Good, happy, wholesome memories overcome by weeds.

Jesus warned that the soil of our hearts is the most valuable property on earth. It is in this soil that we plant good seeds, uproot weeds and harvest fruit for the promotion of His kingdom. Jesus warned of the choking influence of weeds that squeeze the life out of fruit producing seeds. Sin is a deceptive weed that chokes the life from our responsiveness to God. Any experienced farmer will tell you that weeds left unattended can cut the harvest as much as 40 to 60 percent. As is so evident by my example, it takes only a few weeks for the weeds to invade when efforts to control them ceases.

As we consider the consequences of our lives, we need to be intentional about pulling out, poisoning and plowing under the weeds of sin in our lives. As with the golf course, the weeds of sin and disobedience can choke out the good in our lives. Once Jesus becomes a second tier priority, evil is swift to invade. Our souls once manicured by the Holy Spirit are now weed invested jungles.

So .... how do we control the weeds??? The Psalmist prays, "Oh search me God and know my heart; try me and know my thoughts to see if there is any wickedness (weeds) in me". First we must see our sinfulness (weeds) and recognize it for what it is. It's so easy to sugar coat our small habitual sins or seek loopholes to rationalize inappropriate lifestyles. Truth is, there is no magical herbicide to eradicate the weeds of sin from our lives. Only through a relationship with Jesus Christ comes the hope for a weed free life manicured by the Holy Spirit. Happy gardening!!!

TALK IS CHEAP

There are many things in this world easier to talk about than to actually do. Let's say shooting a round of golf with a score of 70 as an example. Such an endeavor is easy for me to talk about. I can talk with confidence about birdies, eagles, bogeys and pars. Trouble is, or should I say fact of the matter is, actually accomplishing such a feat is impossible for me. I simply lack the skill. Maybe I have the desire and willingness but my level of ability is not such that my score card will read 70 or anywhere close.

So I can't shoot a 70. Why .... is it lack of practice? Is it lack of priority? How many things in my life have I put before my golf game? The answer to that question is evident and obvious in my actual performance on the course. Rubber meeting the road kinda thing .... and it ain't pretty. Well, enough about golf. I could have used many other examples but my golf proficiency is a clear cut example of an area in my life where I fall extremely short.

What I do want to talk about is forgiveness. Forgiveness is one of the most prominent themes in our lives as followers of Jesus. We all need it and are expected to offer it. How good are we at it? How often do we practice it? Like my golf score, do we fall short because we don't practice it and fail to place a high priority setting on it in our lives? Fact is, forgiveness does not come easy for most of us. Most of us just don't naturally overflow with love, mercy, grace and understanding. Forgiveness cuts across the natural tendency to hate or seek revenge against those who have wronged us. Is forgiveness a conscious choice or an emotional state of being?

God's word offers insight. "Bear with each other and forgive whatever grievances you may have against one another. Forgive as the Lord forgave you (Colossians 3:13). These words make it crystal clear that we are called to forgive others out of obedience to God. Peter seemed to be have questions relative to forgiveness and God addressed him in one of the most profound statements on forgiveness in the Bible found in Matthew 18:21. "Lord, how many times shall I forgive my brother when he sins against me? Up to seven times?" Jesus responded with words that clarify the "absoluteness" of forgiveness when He answered, "I tell you, not seven times, but seventy-seven times."

Lewis Smedes writes in his book, Forgive and Forget, "When you release the wrongdoer from the wrong, you cut a malignant tumor out of your inner life. You set a prisoner free." Failure to set free the prisoner makes you the prisoner. We are incapable of embracing the perfection of God without realizing the imperfection of ourselves as people. We as imperfect people make decisions sometimes that hurt ourselves and the ones who love us. We as imperfect people are in need of second chances. Imperfect people make mistakes. One of which should not be refusing to offer through the act of forgiveness a redemptive second chance to others.

WHATS IN YOUR BAG

Consider all the clubs you have in your bag. Acording to the USGA, a golfer is allowed to have 14 clubs in his bag. This may include three woods (driver, 3-wood and 5-wood), eight irons, (3-9 iron and pitching wedge), and putter. Some golfers travel light, some are loaded for bear.

Club manufacturers spend millions each year on variations to the older standard. One popular newer concept is the HYBRID. The Hybrid design borrows from both irons and woods while differing from both. Over 30% of recreational golfers report using at least one hybrid club with 65% of pros carrying at least one or more hybrid clubs in their bags. Point being: technology has loaded up the golf bags of players with clubs, range finders and gadgets designed to (at least they want us to believe will) make us better golfers with lower scores.

If you met Jesus on the golf course today, what clubs would He see in your spiritual bag? Is there love, compassion, forgiveness, hope and grace? Is there jealousy, hatred, sin and deceit? What is your established character, demeanor and attitude as you navigate the course of life?

Regardless of the clubs you might choose or the techniques you employ, your final score is all that matters. God takes great delight in our lives being filled with the things that please and glorify HIM and show love and forgiveness to others.

ADVICE FROM AN OLD HACKER

Regardless of distance – Hit the ball straight.

Life is simpler when you avoid the bunkers.

Forgive your enemies; it messes up their heads.

Great device guaranteed to cut five strokes off your score …… an eraser.

Don't judge a golfer by his equipment.

The WORST day on the golf course beats the heck out of the BEST day at work.

REMEMBER …. It's just a game.

Letting' the cat outta the bag is a whole lot easier than puttin' it back in.

Live simply. Love generously. Care deeply. Speak kindly. Leave the rest to God.

Don't pick a fight with an old golfer. If he is too old to fight, he'll just shoot you.

Most times, it just gets down to common sense.

DIMPLES AND ALL

Gotta share this one with you by way of Phil Callaway. There are approximately 400 dimples in a golf ball. If you remove those dimples, the ball would only travel 60 to 80 yards when struck by the club. As surely as a golf ball needs these indentations, the trials of life deepen us and put our character to the test. Difficult times can bring out the worst in us, but when we choose joy, embrace courage, and follow Jesus, they can help us discover the very best God has for us.

We all love mountaintop experiences, but we don't grow there. Life's larger lessons are learned most often through tough times. The trials of life also prepare us to help those who are experiencing difficulty. Second Corinthians 1:4 teaches that God comforts us in all our troubles so that we can comfort others.

Give thanks to the only God who consoles us in all our affliction, so that we may be able to console those who are in any affliction with the consolation with which we ourselves are consoled ..... 2 Corinthians 1:4. If you are suffering - there is hope that at the end of the darkness. With Jesus, you will be stronger in your faith and better equipped to shine your light of God's love with the world.

ALBERT

Traded a chain of e-mails last week with my buddy Albert Long. He had asked me to help out in arranging a speaking engagement for a friend of his. I gotta tell you, Albert is a character. While I will not disclose his age, (sure he wouldn't mind if I did) this guy has more energy and passion for spreading the word of Jesus Christ than any man I have ever met. I know of NO man fifty years his junior that can cover Prince Albert. It's just in his DNA.

Seems it was hard to cover Albert on the basketball court, football, baseball and track field as well. Albert is the only four sport letterman in the history of the Atlantic Coast Conference. This man is a maniac. I am always better after I talk with him or receive one of his straightforward notes. He is a cherished friend even though he's a Tarheel.

Anyway ...... I just finished my third book of devotionals and was chatting with Albert last week in that regard as well. He was kind enough to pen the Forward to the book which is quite an honor for me. Albert always has someone on his mind and last week it was local grown PGA Masters Champ Webb Simpson. Albert and Webb are connected through The Fellowship of Christian Athletes. Albert is a FCA Hall of Champion recipient and Webb will surely be in that group one day.

I had the pleasure of meeting Simpson a few years back at a FCA event. He is quite an impressive young man of God and not a bad golfer.

Albert was telling me about Webb's favorite bible verse being James 1:2-4. "Dear brothers and sisters, whenever trouble comes your way, let it be an opportunity for joy. For when your faith is tested, your endurance has a chance to grow. So let it grow, for when your endurance is fully developed, you will be strong in character and ready for anything."

I guess if you reach a level of celebrity in life such as Simpson and still remain faithful to God, then you have seen a lot of trouble. Albert assures me that Webb is as strong in his commitment to God as he is in his golf game. To that I say: "Praise God." We need more men like Webb Simpson in professional sports.

The writer of this passage was James, the half brother of Jesus. In the passage, James does not say "if" trouble comes your way but "when" it does. We hear the message that "when" we have troubles, it is possible to profit from them. James suggests that we turn our hardships into times of reflection and learning. Kinda like modern day Nike theology: "no pain - no gain."

I will even suggest that our true character is reveled through our pain. It is only human to ask "why" or "where is God" during times of trouble but I believe that God is more interested in making us mature and complete in our faith than keeping us from pain and sadness. I think it's important to see trouble through these lenses or else we have no port of hope during our storms.

I celebrate my friendship with Albert Long. God put him on my path last week with a message that I needed to hear at a time I needed to hear it. It's a message we all need to hear and attempt to understand and believe. It's a message to use now if you are in a valley or to tuck away in a safe place for the storm that "will" blow into your life. As a favorite teacher of mine used to say: (and frequently I must add) "this is a good time to pay attention".

GREAT GOLFER – LOVING DAD

Hobbies are an essential element for a balanced life. They are an oasis from the stress and responsibilities of everyday life. I have several hobbies. One of my favorite warm season hobbies is golf. I enjoy being outdoors spending time with good friends and family. The competitive challenge of the game for me is relaxing. Seven percent of golfers play the game left handed. I am in that minority along with two of my favorite golfers Phil Mickelson and Bubba Watson. Bubba was probably my number one favorite until last week.

It was announced last week that Phil Mickelson will skip the upcoming U.S. Open to attend his daughter Amanda's graduation from high school. When asked about the decision Mickelson replied, "As I look back on life, this is a moment I'll always cherish and be glad I was present. There's no greater joy as a parent." Those who follow the game know that Mickelson has won five major championships including three Masters green jackets but has never won the U.S. Open. He has finished in second place six times, more than any other player in history. You gotta believe that Mickelson wants this championship that has eluded him not to mention the $2.16 million pay day for the winner.

I am now even a bigger fan of Mickelson. His decision was loving, caring, sensitive, self-effacing, gracious and responsible. Selfishness runs rampant in our "it's all about me" culture. We can care excessively for our own advantage, pleasure and welfare while many times showing total disregard for others. Philippians 2:4 warns that we are to look not only to our own interest but also to the interest of others. Paul encourages us to guard against any selfishness that might lead to dissension. Showing genuine interest in people other than ourselves is a positive step in maintaining unity among others.

According to Forbes, Mickelson is one of the richest athletes in the world. Since his pro career was born in 1992, Mickelson has earned over $80 Million in PGA prize money. Aside from his PGA income, Mickelson earned over $50 Million in 2016 off the course from sponsors, appearances and course design work. His Net Worth has been approximated over $300 Million.

My point here with the money is that papa Mickelson could have bought his daughter any graduation gift she desired. Instead he chose to give her the greatest gift a father can give a child ...... his time.

HACKER

You don't have to be in many conversations about golf before you hear the term Hacker. According to Wikipedia "Hacker" is something no golfer ever wants to be called. Hacker is a derogatory term in golf that refers to someone who rarely plays golf and as a result is quite bad when they do; generally, any golfer who is just not very good at it; a mediocre or poor golfer who displays bad golf etiquette and/or poor sportsmanship.

WOW .. sounds like a ruthless character to say the least. After a little thought on the subject I realized that I once was a hacker in the realm of golf. Over time my score and knowledge of the game has improved and hopefully I am edging away from that dreaded label. After a few lessons and a dedication to playing more, I am more confident and much less intimated on the course.

You know ..... in God's eyes we all are "hackers". We are taught in scripture that we ALL have fallen short of the glory of God. A sinful nature is born into each of us. Although our actions may be appropriate, God knows our every thought. He knows all our motives and agendas. He see us when we are hidden from the world. He knows our hearts.

It is only due to HIS grace that we, in all our shortcomings, are welcomed into HIS presence. No amount of money can purchase that for you. No action or any deed you might perform can gain you a verdict of not guilty. All is needed is an act of humbleness and admission that we are in fact a "Hacker" and accept the fact that God is our Lord and Savior. His mighty gift of salvation and grace will handle the rest. Jesus has our back and the tab has already been paid.

Next time you witness a Hacker on the course or become maybe a little frustrated with less than "par" performance from another player, remember Jesus. Exercise HIS model of grace and understanding. Pay if forward !!!!

PLAY YOUR GAME

I have a good friend I play with often whose game is much stronger than my own. He has played the game of golf for over forty years and his score is evidence of the fact. He has played some of the finest courses and has developed a wealth of knowledge and talent.

Whenever we tee it up, he can sometimes sense my frustration with my skill level not being up to par with his own. He is fond of saying: "Cha (he calls me Cha) don't worry about me or anybody else. Play your own game."

I was frustrated because I was trying to play his game and I couldn't. That frustration was ruining my game. He showed me that it's OK to play my game along side of his game. Yes his drives were longer, and his shots more accurate than mine, but that had nothing to do with my game. If I play my game, I'll play better and in time I'll improve. As time has passed my game improved, but at my own pace. I enjoy my game and challenge myself to succeed.

God has given each of us our own game and calling in life. Sometimes we get caught up trying to compete with others and become frustrated with what we fear is a lack of success. You can never win your game by playing somebody else's. Be the best with your game and you'll grow with satisfaction.

God has you right where you are for HIS purpose. He has put you there because you are the best choice for your game.

IN THE DITCH

I have used the term "in the ditch" all my life. Since I started playing golf, my version of "in the ditch" has become "in the bunker". Bunkers are a normal part of any golf course. They are in fact much more than a "ditch". They are scattered indentions in the course filled with sand. Deep and wide holes with nearly vertical walls. I have spent my fair share of time in the bunker.

Like the ditch, once you find yourself there, you gotta get out. There is a technique for doing so. First, you need to stabilize your feet so they are solid in the spongy sand. Using the proper club (sand wedge) you open your stance and make sure to swing all the way through the ball. Because bunkers are filled with sand, the footing can be tricky. Sand is definitely not a firm foundation on which to hit a golf ball or build a house. See Matthew 7:24-27 for more on that subject.

Living in the world today can be akin to getting out of a bunker. As we face the shifting sands of this unstable, ever changing world, it's important that we develop a firm footing in our faith. We need to be grounded in the truth of God's Word. It doesn't change, it is rock solid. As followers of Jesus, we trust in the firm footing of God's word. Strange as it may sound, but to hit a ball out of bunker you need to strike the sand behind and under the ball instead of the ball itself. This way you'll get the loft you need to bring the ball out of the bunker and on to the green.

GET A GRIP

My son and I recently started a new hobby as if we don't have enough on our plates. We have taken up re-gripping golf clubs. We began by purchasing a vise to hold the clubs in place, a special knife to remove the old grips, grip tape and last but not least solvent. We have re-gripped all our own clubs and some for our friends.

The grip is a very important component of any golf club whether it is a driver, iron, wedge or putter. Grips come in different sizes and designs. The size or circumference is important because the hands of golfers vary in size. Both my son and I have XX Large hands so we use the jumbo size grips on our clubs. The texture of the grip is also important. Grips vary in feel ranging from smooth to varying degrees of texture.

We have heard the phrase all our life "Get A Grip". This conveys one to relax; to calm down; to stop being angry; to come to one's senses or become more rational. He needs to get a grip if he's getting that angry over such a little thing.

Like a golf club, we need a proper "grip" on our lives. We need a solid base of contact with reality that guides our actions, motives and attitudes. Sometimes we squeeze a little tighter to "hang on" to our lives.

Having an appropriate grip on our lives, like the golf club, is a key element in the direction our lives (the ball in case of the club) will travel. Some days are par threes and others are par fives. Some days we experience more bunkers and ponds than others.

An appropriate grip on our lives helps to establish a rhythm to which we can navigate both the good and bad days. There are always folks who threaten to steal our joy. A proper grip allows us to deal with circumstances that might otherwise upset us or throw us off balance. Once we establish the proper grip, life becomes easier and less dramatic.

Practice your grip. Learn to take the good with the bad. Learn that most obstacles in life CAN be overcome .... with the right grip.

GIVE ME A MULLIGAN

My latest life passion is conquering the game of golf. I bought a set of clubs back in the 80's, played a few rounds and stuffed them in the closet fed up, disgusted and frustrated. Well, I am back in the game. Got a new updated set of clubs and not one but two golf coaches. Progress is being made but it ain't pretty. My youngest son is a golfer. The major motivation in my renewed interest in the game is to be able to play with him in the years to come. My current goal is to get my score into double figures (IE: 99 versus 130).

Immediately after I jumped back in the fray, I learned there are thousands, not hundreds, of gizmos, gadgets, and devices guaranteed to lower your score. I can testify to this because I now own half of them. I have graphite shafts on my irons, non-slip grips on my drivers, custom lofts on my wedges and a balanced head putter guaranteed to sink the ball every time. There are driving nets, putting mats and weighted training clubs. I have had my swing videoed, analyzed, tweaked and corrected. I am paying ridiculous money to be advised, taught, equipped and coached. And you know what ……. it is still the most frustrating endeavor I have ever attempted.

Truth is all the gadgets and gimmicks don't work. Even my two coaches disagree on some very basic elements of the game. I have come to realize the only way I am going to learn this game of golf is to commit to practice, follow the advice I am given and be patient. In other words ..... "live it." It is apparent that reaching the level of play I desire is going to take some time. Regardless of what the gadget peddlers promise, there is no easy way or shortcut.

As believers, sometimes I wonder if we over promise the life ahead once we make a decision to live our life for Christ. There are certainly some that preach an over the top gospel of prosperity. When we read of the miracles Jesus performed, do we put all our cards in the basket of hope that a miracle will come our way? Do we expect a life free of loss and pain once we walk the aisle to salvation?

Fact is, our lives in this world are much akin to my current golf game ...... "broken". From the moment we enter this fallen world, we begin to decay and break down. There is pain wrapped around death, sickness and hurt found in the challenges of friends and family. There is loss around every corner as we maneuver through our life with all the worldly responsibilities and relationships.

I have played in a couple of charity golf events recently and immediately developed an appreciation for mulligans. A mulligan is when a player gets a second chance to make a shot. A mulligan, simply put, is a "do over". Hit a bad shot? Take a mulligan and replay the stroke. Mulligans are not "legal" under the rules of golf but offered as a friendly gesture in charity tournaments and fundraising events. Heck !!! you have to pay for mulligans.

Good thing God is not a golfer. He freely offers mulligans in the form of his grace and gift of salvation. A second chance is not only legal in God's play book but is the essential theme in his invitation to each of us to live our lives for HIM. As with my golf game, there is hope for my life. However in that hope comes a responsibility of commitment to learn and live the game .... and yes, I'll take a mulligan or two along the way. For further information on God's mulligan, see John 3:16.

FIRM FOUNDATION

I know there have been times when you were forced to hit a shot from the rough, fringe or bunker. Not a shot from the nice, solid, even and firm foundation of the fairway. A good golf shot is a challenging endeavor under the best conditions but what about when our footing and foundation is not good.

I know you know where I headed with this one. When things in our life are based on the firm foundation of a personal relationship with Jesus, the shots we are called on to make are much easier. If we are swinging atop a firm foundation, it is more likely the ball is going to go where we desire.

In golf terms we dread a "Bare Lie" when the ball lies directly on hard ground without any grass to buoy the ball up. There is no grass creating a gap between ball and the ground making a desirable shot more difficult.

The shots we make on the course and in our lives are more accurate from a firm foundation. Following the firm foundation laid by Jesus will equip us to avoid the bunkers and traps of life. When that foundation is not in our lives – when we have chosen to chase some temptation or rely on something other than God's Word – we tend to lose our grip on the things that are really most important in life and to God.

FINDING THE LINE

Ask any golfer and they will agree that putting is the most challenging aspect of their game. Improve your putting and your score will improve. Makes sense. One of the more challenging aspects of putting is that the ball remains on the ground. Your tee shot and approach shots all fly in the air.

It's only when we arrive on the green that the ground becomes a factor. All greens differ in design, elevation and slope. Depending on their current condition, they may be fast or slow. These conditions affect the speed the ball travels thus affecting the amount of force you need to apply when striking the ball.

Because no greens are flat, they take on an individual character of their own. In order to put the ball in the cup, you first must determine the line. The line is the direction the ball must travel to the cup. If the green slopes to the right, you'll need to hit the ball to the left of the hole to compensate for the slope. The successful golfer never aims directly for the cup. Instead you aim for the fall point of the line where the ball will break for the cup.

Our lives are a lot like putting greens. We each have our own lines. Some of us struggle with issues that affect our personal landscapes. We all have our own special idiosyncrasies. Each life has a line. These lines in our lives affect the way we interact with others.

These lines comprise our sensitivities. Like finding the line when we putt, it's important to consider the lines running within the relationships with others.

No matter how the outside appears, everyone has issues and struggles. It's important that we extend love and grace towards the people of which we interact.

A DAY OF GIVING

It was a beautiful day. The sun was shining and the air was "fall like" crisp. Early morning brought a swell of activity as members of Banded Brothers were preparing to welcome 31 teams to our 8th annual charity golf tournament. Today was a day set aside to serve the Lord through serving our neighbors? While the ground was still soaked with the morning's dew, my brothers were shuffling to plant over 100 sponsor signs. Others were busy with registration duties alongside those who were stocking the beverage cart and packing box lunches.

It's quite a divine moment when you find yourself immersed in service. I often struggle with the reality of the time I waste in nothing more than self serving activities, but not on this day. This is a day for our brothers to face the reality of our blessings and the responsibility we have as followers of Jesus to serve the Lord by serving others.

The Bible teaches us that we are blessed not just to feel good, be happy or comfortable but to also bless others. God told Abraham, "I will bless you and you will be a blessing." God promises that if we will concentrate on blessing others, He will take care of our needs. In Luke 12:48, Jesus informs us that "Much is required from the person to whom much is given; Much more is required from the person to whom much more is given." Those who were with us on this day have been abundantly blessed beyond anything we deserve and together we celebrate the presence to give back to others less fortunate.

Every penny of the over $23,000 raised on this day will be used in our local communities to help those with some sort of need. Last year *Banded Brothers* funded three burials, built over 300 infant cradles, assisted a half dozen folks buried under medical bills and sent a young lady to college who would not, under no other circumstances, been able to become the first person in her family to attend college. Many of these people we do not know nor will ever meet. We work through a referral process fueled by, what we believe to be, divine intervention. Red tape, committees and bureaucratic nonsense will not be found in our mission statement.

It's an eerie directive, bound in reality, we find in Mark 14:7, "You will always have the needy among you." We all are living sacrifices giving the things God has given us by giving to others. In that, we find life. God, the giver of all things, gives us everything we need to fulfill His will. By day's end , we had 124 spent golfers and many exhausted helpers that had answered that call. Freely we have received, freely we will give.

BE A GO-GIVER

Our annual golf tournament always reminds me of the blessing afforded my soul in being a member of *Banded Brothers*. God has showered me with opportunities to stand in the gap with some of my best buddies to help others that find themselves falling through the cracks of life. We are not the United Way or Salvation Army. We have no highly paid millionaire executives (or any paid folks for that matter) nor do we work through red tape or bureaucratic channels. We are intentionally just people helping people.

I do so enjoy reviewing the cards and letters received throughout the year from the individuals and families that we have assisted. The notes and letters are filed in a binder and it seems I never complete review of its contents without having to reach for a Kleenex. This can be very powerful stuff. Coming alongside others when they are down and seemingly without hope has to be one of the most genuine, revealing and fully transparent experience of service. Receiving these expressions of appreciation is not why we do what we do but they do afford a blessing back to our group that fuels our enthusiasm to keep on keeping on.

Jesus said, If you give a cup of water to someone in need, you will surely be rewarded. Our love for God can be measured how well we treat others. God is aware of every deed we do or don't do as if He was the one receiving it. Every time you reach out to another, every time you go out of your way to make someone's pain a little more bearable ...... God sees it. There may be no worldly applause and that's OK. As God's people, we don't need applause. There is no need for a crowd cheering us on. We don't need a plague or award to hang on the wall. Service to those less fortunate is a spiritual principle.

Whatever we give will be given back to us with interest. What we make happen for others .... God will make happen for us. To each *Banded Brother* I say thank you for your friendship. I am proud to STAND by your side. And thanks to all who have supported our causes. And above all remember the best part ..... God appreciates it as well !!!!!

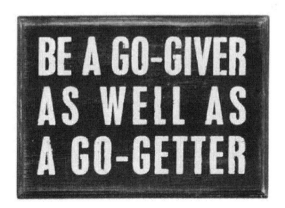

IN HER OWN WORDS

Thanks to all the golfers who have played and participated in our annual golf tournament for the past twelve years. Below is an unedited note that was sent to me written by a lady in our area whose son was recently gunned down in a gang related incident. This young man had just come to the Lord through a prison ministry that our organization, *Banded Brothers*, supports. There is nothing I can add. Her words are clearly spoken from the heart with a message we all need to hear.

Have you ever felt like giving up or throwing in the towel? We all have been there but always; right when it seems like it can't get any worse somebody says something to encourage you or perhaps an unexpected door opens and you find yourself strengthened from within. On January 5th 2011, my 18 yr son was shot in the head as he walked with friends. I had actually just rode past him on my way home, as soon as I pulled in the driveway, I heard gun fire and immediately a cold chill went through me.

Needless to say my world was turned upside down. The doctors and nurses all told me that it was hopeless; they didn't expect him to survive and even suggested that I end care. I was told by one of the doctors that I should end care because my son was not able to breathe on his own this was on a Monday, I will never forget it. My response to that doctor was "I believe God and that's not what God told me"; that following Friday; they took my son off the ventilator and he's been breathing on his own ever since.

Had I believed that doctor over God my son would be dead today. Choose to believe God no matter what your circumstances are telling you. Yes it looked bad for my son by all accounts but remember it's not based on how a thing looks but by what God says; his word has the final authority.

Speak the word of God today. Believe that your situation is going to get better regardless of how it looks or feel. My son came home from the hospital on June 3rd 2011; he has his memory, he is in his right mind and I know that he will be completely restored.

Be blessed and know that God never slumbers nor sleep his eyes go to and fro throughout the earth searching for someone to show kindness to. Today is your day.

SUPERBALL

Superball also known as captains choice or scramble is a format where all players on a team hit from the tee, select the best shot, everyone hits from there, select the best shot, and on and on until the ball is holed. This format is commonly used in tournament play to lure unskilled players into the mix. Regardless of your skill level, you can be on the winning team if other members of your team can pick up the slack.

Superball also tends to take some pressure off an individual's game and provide a more enjoyable atmosphere such as the one you might intend to establish in tournament play. It cultivates a deeper sense of team play, strategy and comradery. I play in several super ball tournaments each year and enjoy the concept. How else am I going to tab a score below sixty five?

Seems to me that we need a little more "super ball" in our relationships with one another. Each of us have our special and unique God given gifts and talents. Some of us are better putters while others drive the ball further while still others have a tighter short game.

The opportunities in our lives to contribute to the welfare of others should always be seen as an opportunity to bless another human being. We are all in this game of life together. If I can assist in the advancement of my brother, then I must seize that opportunity.

All the technology and advancements in our world today lend to isolation. The interdependency that folks faced years ago has evaporated. No one wants to get involved. No one wants to tend to another's business. What happened to the Sunday afternoon visits with neighbors that I remember as a child?

Why don't we all try to play a little more "super ball" with those around us? Let's offer up our good shots to others while being willing to accept those offered to us.

YOU ARE A RINGER

There's a term you might hear when talking golf. This term will likely be in the context of team tournament play. The term is "ringer". Maybe you have heard the term. Maybe you are one. One formal definition reads: Ringer – individual used to bolster the quality of the performance and increase the pleasure of performers especially in amateur groups. There isn't necessarily a negative connotation associated with the term or even its use.

My personal experience with ringers has been associated with super ball tournaments. On the day of the tournament folks are arriving, equipment is being loaded in carts and team members are assembling. You approach a group you know …. well except for this stranger. As you greet your friends, the stranger is introduced as a third, half, step, long lost cousin from Cincinnati. At that moment you know something is up. The smell of a rat permeates the air.

I will not hesitate to proclaim each of us "ringers" in our own special and particular way. We each have our field of expertise and can outperform others relative to our talents. There is something another in this world can do better than you. Some are scratch golfers and others know how to program a remote.

This is why community is so very important in our lives. The dependency and interdependency we have on others is the thread that weaves the fabric of life. It does take a village. I have no desire to learn the backside of my computer but I am thankful for my friend Dave who does.

ALWAYS REMEMBER THAT

* A golf match is a test of your skill against your opponents luck.

* Counting on your opponent to inform you when he breaks a rule is like expecting him to make fun of his own haircut.

* The shortest distance between any two points on a golf course is a straight line that passes directly through the center of a very large tree.

* There are two kinds of bounces; unfair bounces and bounces just the way you meant to play it.

* You can hit a two acre fairway 10% of the time and a two-inch branch 90% of the time.

* If you want to hit a 7 iron as far as Tiger Woods does, simply try to lay up just short of a water hazard.

* Never try to keep more than 300 separate thoughts in your mind during your swing.

* When your shot has to carry over a water hazard, you can either hit one more club or two more balls.

* You can put "draw" on the ball, you can put "fade" on the ball, but no golfer can put "straight" on the ball.

* Never buy a putter until you've had a chance to throw it.

BE A DOER

Human nature is a funny thing. There are so many tendencies we posses as broken people with a sinful nature. Look no further than the book of Titus where Paul encourages the true believers to stand strong. Many people in that time were all talk and didn't live up to their words, especially when it came to Christ. Paul called these kinds of people despicable, disobedient and worthless for doing anything good. Sounds kinda harsh there Paul.

Ever heard someone brag about their golf game? Ever known anyone who lied about their handicap? There is much spoken on the 19th hole that can't be produced on the previous 18. We read in the first chapter of the book of James: do not just talk or listen to the word, be doers of it. Christ said that if you are going to tell Him you love Him, also show Him. Peter showed us a prime example of a cheap talker. His heart was good, but he did not always walk his talk and did not show Christ that his talk was a reflection of his true belief. We all are guilty on these terms.

A parent wants to believe that their children will do what they say all the time. But they know that that is not always the case. Those parents who can convince their children to talk less and do more will usually find a greater level of success. Jesus wants the same for His children. He wants us to talk less about all the great things we intend to do for Him and to start doing them. He wants a lifestyle of action, not just of mere talk. Talk is cheap, and action is everything.

GRACE FILLED UNDERSTANDING

Hands down ... my favorite golfer is Bubba Watson. He's a family man, never taken any formal golf lessons, is left handed and has that "southern" flair that I can easily identify with. My admiration for Bubba was enhanced further after watching a 60 Minutes story on Bubba. The story showed an honest and vulnerable side of him. Although Bubba has fans like me, not everyone roots for him. Known for his outbursts and how he treats his caddie, he's not regarded as the friendliest guy on tour. Word around the clubhouse is Bubba isn't even well-liked by other golfers. With all this considered, many come to his defense.

Even his caddie, who is the victim of Mr. Watson's short fuse, defended his boss. The caddie, Ted Scott, said: "People don't like Bubba and...the reason why they don't him is they just don't understand him because he's nuts." I think there is a compliment buried in there somewhere from someone who should know this man well and spends a lot of time by his side.

Bubba admitted he has a lot of emotional issues. He doesn't do well around large crowds. That's not a good problem to have when you are a celebrity. What struck me most about the story was his revelation that he's been misunderstood. There is no justification for his temper tantrums or the struggles he has with people, but I am willing to show him grace in recognizing he acts the way he does because of what lies beneath the surface. I think we all have similar issues. I know I am very often misunderstood..

This type of understanding is at best difficult at times. It doesn't come easy for most of us. We tend to jump to conclusions and judge others from the outside when voicing our opinion about not liking them. The simple reality is that people are the way they are for a reason. That doesn't mean they should stay as they are, but it also doesn't mean we should write them off. I have enough hope in mankind to believe that most people are genuinely good and mean well in their actions.

The divine elasticity due others is supported in Proverbs 18:2 hearing great wisdom with these words: "Fools have no interest in understanding; they only want to air their own opinions." I believe this is valuable in many areas of life, but today let's be challenged to do our best to understand people before giving our assessment of them. We all have our own struggles, issues, and hurts, so let's love each other and remember that Jesus meets us in our brokenness.

EASY DOES IT

One of the most difficult lessons for a new golfer to learn is to swing nice and easy with a loose and relaxed grip. What ????? if I am supposed to drive the ball 250 yards down the middle of the fairway I've got to crush it. The general tendency for a rookie player is to "grip it and rip it". As with many things in life, we find that big results can be gleaned from slow and controlled technique.

As we age and mature in the things of the world, we tend to slow down. Each mile further down the road we travel, we gain wisdom and power in our faith. I testify and confirm the words of John 10:27, "My sheep listen to my voice; I know them, and they follow me."

 Further, Jeremiah 2:25 speaks about this hurried dilemma: Slow down. Take a deep breath. What's the hurry? Why wear yourself out? Just what are you after anyway? Understanding God's presence in our lives and being still enough to sense it are two different things. We must slow down and quiet ourselves long enough to fully hear Him.

God is in constant conversation with those who know Him. He whispers to our soul. Silent commands of what to do, say or not say are always present. But in our hurriedness, we often fail to hear.   Slowing down and prioritizing God will help us to hear His voice more clearly. I now know Him more and encourage others to as well. Hearing His whispers has led me to new adventures I could never have known on my own. But first, I needed to be still.

SET YOUR GOALS

When I finally decided to take the game of golf seriously, I had a short bout with frustration. Being competitive at all I do I found it a little difficult not to be able to master the game in a few rounds. Didn't take long for me to realize that becoming competitive at golf would be a long journey. So I immediately modified my strategy.

I knew I had to play often so I joined a club and beefed up my bag with some modern equipment. Next I set a goal. My first goal was to learn to hit the ball straight. Not long but straight. To achieve that goal I took some lessons and played and played and played.

My son was home from college for the summer so I had a partner. He has been playing since he was a kid and was very helpful in sharing his skills and knowledge of the game with me. As my skill level began to ramp up I set a goal of double bogey play. Double bogey would give me two extra strokes per hole beyond par to get that stupid ball in the cup.

Didn't take long before I was consistently achieving my goal and on many days even scoring lower. As I began to learn the basic techniques, my enjoyment of the game increased.

Taking it nice and slow is a basic reality when learning a new skill. This golf adventure reminded quite often of the journey I began deciding to become a follower of Jesus some

twenty years ago. At first we are on fire for the 'word". We sign up for every Bible study, participate in every mission opportunity and fully immerse ourselves in this new way of life we have embraced. And that is good.

As we settle in this new game, it's doesn't take long to recognize that it will be a journey. God's salvation is free and not based on works. We realize the important of curbing our enthusiasm in a way to refine and improve our performance. It's important to allow all the new information and experiences to slowly sink in.

As we proclaim ourselves followers of Jesus we are there center stage to all in our sphere of influence to see.

WISDOM

By now you just might be tired of hearing folks declare their New Year resolutions. Exhaustion may even be upon you in defining your own. However, here's two more for you. My first resolution is to develop my golf game. No real eternal benefit to a lower golf score but I enjoy the game and being with my buddies. The second resolution is to more intentionally "seek wisdom."

Webster defines "wisdom" as the " knowledge that is gained by having many life experiences." Well, I got plenty of those over my years. I can relate to that definition, however I am better connecting with the one Andy Stanley offers in his book, *Guardrails*. Stanley considers wisdom as "knowing right from wrong and choosing to do what is right." I like that and am convinced that I need more of that in my life.

There is a stark two fold directive found in Proverbs 13:20 relative to wisdom. Goes something like this: "Walk with the wise and become wise, for a companion of fools suffers harm." After reading Stanley's book, wisdom for me takes on less about being intelligent. I don't intend to judge here, but there are plenty of highly intelligent folks walking around that are not "wise" enough to do the right things in life. Takes me back to the "mad scientist" we read about in comic books in our youth.

What is being suggested in the verse from Proverbs is if you connect with wise folks, you are more likely to become wise yourself. That's fairly straight forward. The later part of the verse suggests if you connect with foolish folks you might not necessarily become a fool BUT you may suffer negative consequences because of the company you have chosen to keep. Eventually the shrapnel from the life of a fool can and will impact others in the line of fire.

Slippery slope here because we know Jesus hung out with the "undesirables" (fools) but He was not shaped by their actions. His mission was to transform not inaugurate. Wisdom, or lack thereof, greatly influences the direction and spiritual quality of our lives. Scripture (Proverbs 4:6-7) instructs us not to forsake wisdom, it will protect us, it will watch over us. Wisdom is supreme; therefore get it. That's my plan. I'll handle the golf game - wish me luck on the wisdom journey.

WHERE YOU TRAVELING ???

I live on five acres. Two acres were cleared for my house and lawn with the remainder left heavily wooded and full of wildlife. I was hitting golf balls in my yard last week aiming towards a practice net. The net prevents the balls from winding up in the woods. It may be hard to believe but a few balls missed the net. That is why I am practicing. After my practice session, I walked into the woods to retrieve the golf balls that mysteriously missed the net. It's important that the stray balls are retrieved or else they will be found in the jaws of my bulldog.

As I walked into the woods searching for balls, I noticed there were very obvious paths cut in the underbrush. These paths, 18 to 24 inches wide, wove throughout my property and continued on across to my neighbor's property. Upon further investigation, I discovered the path floor was covered in deer tracks. These paths had been cut by the deer herds that frequent our area. These ruts, cut deep within the thick forest, were evidence of the direction the herds took as they navigated from place to place. Being curious, I followed the path until it leads to a stream that runs across the rear of our neighborhood. In an open area, the brush was pressed and matted into shapes that appeared to be sites where the deer bedded down for the night.

The routes of these paths were cut deep into the woods far away from the homes built in our neighborhood. For the most, they followed the flow and slope of the terrain as though intentional plans had been laid for their creation. Their flow and design seemed to suggest some planning and forethought. I know what you're thinking; deer don't think .... well maybe they do. The design and location of these paths of travel seemed to suggest that seclusion and safety from humans were the key elements of their construction.

Later as I pondered my discovery, I begin to think about my faith paths. Where do I travel? Do I choose to travel along a path that will ensure I not pass by someone who might threaten me or may not be like me? Do I take the safe route as opposed to another direction that may present a greater level of risk taking? Do I travel the familiar path that secures me from meeting others that might need or demand something of me? Have I become complacent on my path and lost the adventure of faith sharing that Gods calls me to?

What I do know is Jesus followed no specific path nor did he view any place or any person outside his reach. Jesus followed a path of spontaneity. He never chose not to walk towards those who were lost, beat or broken. The path Jesus followed was not rutted and worn like the path of the deer. It was a risky path less traveled. It was a path that leads him to death on a cross cut from rough timbers. It is because of the path that Jesus followed, that we have a path. A path that will lead us to eternity. A safe and secure path like the path of the deer. It is with that security that we find the courage to wander into the lives of folks that surround us. Folks not on our path. Folks who need to hear about the One whose path we follow. Where is your path leading you?

OPEN YOUR EYES AND SEE HIS BEAUTY

One great aspect about the game of golf is that it's played outdoors in a natural environment. The are no chalked boundary lines or bases spiked in the ground. Even the same course can be greatly altered one day to the next by placement of the tees and pins. Maybe only cyclists can appreciate the diversity of their playing grounds as we do as golfers.

The wonders of creation—including those on and around golf courses are perfect reminders of the hand of God. Even creation, we know from Paul's words to the Romans, is groaning for the full coming of Christ's kingdom, but we know as well that "the heavens declare the glory of God" (Psalm 19:1) and "mountains and all hills, fruit trees and cedars" are called upon to sing God's praises (Psalm 148:9).

The course I play most often is covered with hundreds of huge crepe myrtles. When in bloom they provide a heavenly backdrop to the landscape. Next time you tee it up, keep your eyes open for the wondrous works of the hand of God. The beauty of God is stunning. It leaves us in awe. It is God's intense desire that we seek him, see him, and know him in all his beauty. And while you're at it – hit it long and straight.

BAD WEATHER – GREAT DAY

I, along with over one hundred other folks, skipped work last Monday and drove around in golf carts chasing balls in the pouring rain. We were participating in the annual *Banded Brothers* Golf Tournament. This is a day, the first Monday in October, when friends get together to raise money for folks who are less fortunate.

The purpose is helping others, the golf is just a backdrop. Although the weather was terrible for golf, it was a blessed day for giving. By days end, we had raised over $22,000.00. One hundred percent of every dollar will remain in our local communities to assist the victims of social, spiritual and economic disaster.

All those who attended our event have been blessed with wealth to share with those in need. Our local communities are needy places. There are individuals and families that are living on the edge, many in a pure survival mode. Jesus commands those who are able to help. As His followers, we answer that call. This is why we gather in October each year - this is what this event is all about. Paul offers an amazing promise; "You will be made rich in every way so you may be generous on every occasion." Monday was such an occasion. Those who participated believe in that promise.

As Jesus himself put it, having freely received, all disciples are expected to freely give. This directive is reflective of an expectation that the ministry of giving and receiving is part of God's plan for His church in all ages, cultures and economic levels of society. That has been the primary focus of *Banded Brothers* as a charitable organization since its inception. Our people have been made rich in many ways beyond financial resources. On this day each year, we repay a small portion of those blessings. Buying and keeping is not the way of life so we give as often and as much as we can.

Look no further than 2 Corinthians 9:8-14 to hear that charitable giving is not merely a suggestion but a necessary kingdom dynamic. We ought not to be confused nor unclear about where God stands on the matter of giving. His position is made all too clear throughout scripture. God so loved the world that he gave and so must we. In the sunshine - and yes..... in the rain. Wet golf clubs, drenched golfers and all !!!!

BFF

Seems I cannot turn around without seeing or hearing the phrase "BFF". I decided I would conduct my own investigation which uncovered the following facts. "BFF" (Best Friends Forever) is a phrase that describes a close friendship typical of teenage girls and young women. Further research reveals that such friendships are characterized by intimacy, trust and a sense of permanence. It seems these friendships are common in high school but tend to deteriorate when the parties head to college. My research and life experiences conclude that old fogeys like me can also have BFFs.

I had lunch last week with three special friends. Two of them are long time relationships and the other is newfound. One relationship was formed in college and has stood the test of time. This relationship has weathered business deals, divorces, wayward children and about anything you could recall that might challenge a relationship. I truly love this guy and although I'm not a teenage girl or a young woman, he's a BFF in my book and we have the memories to prove it.

Yes, we have the memories to prove it. Memories were the topic of our lunch discussion taking top bill with other guy stuff mixed in such as Tiger Woods and Donald Trump. The other three guys had grown up together in eastern North Carolina and well .... you can imagine the stories. The stories .... yes, that's what brought them back to a greasy spoon diner forty five years later. Looks like some "BFF" going on to me.

Our time was great. The other friend I've known for years has always been a chap I have loved and respected. He was there for me many years ago when I needed a friend and to this day would be there in a second if I needed him. My third friend at the table, I've known for just a short while. I met him through the other two friends. He is a very special man rooted as deep in the spirit of Jesus as anyone I know. He is currently in the process of making some big life decisions. He sat with us and glowed with enthusiasm about how God was setting forth a path for him. You cannot spend too much time around a bro like that.

Finally, I spent the last three days of this week with three other special friends. We chased golf balls through the sandy bottom forests of Pinehurst for three straight days. Like my other friends, we told stories and recounted days gone by .... we laughed a lot. It really feels good to laugh. I'm talking about way down in the gut type laughter. Loved being with these friends. This is an annual thing we do - already looking forward to next year. Did I mention that ..... we laughed a lot? The therapy that a true friend can bring to your life is immeasurable. Do not leave this world with your BFF being your job, bank account or even your dog. Find yourself a BFF by being a BFF .... old guys included !!!!!

OUR JOURNEY TOGETHER

Our journey as *Banded Brothers* has taken our group beyond anything we could have imagined. I am astonished and grateful at what God has allowed us to do over these past 15 years. Space here will not allow me to share about the outreach we have been blessed to be involved in.

Often I ask myself with amazement, "How did it all happen?" From God's side, it was His presence, mercy and grace that went before us and sustained us. And from our side, it was following Him by faith, one step at a time.

Today, people in our communities are shaken by the economy and politics. They live in fear of the future and with uncertainty about their private lives. Fear also seems to be the reason why so many of God's people hesitate to embark on their own journey of faith, especially when He asks them to trust Him for each step they take. They would gladly be willing to invest their lives in winning the lost world for Christ, if only they could see—before they start—how this journey unfolds and ends.

The Lord told Abraham to leave his home and fulfill a specific purpose. God did not spell out the details of his journey or show him a blueprint of the future. Yet Abraham had the God of the future as His friend and guide. And so it has been for *Banded Brothers*.

God had a blueprint for our journey and an annual Golf Tournament was a huge part. Those who have played and given their time and money have impacted the lives of people they will never meet. God has shown us what can be accomplished if we believe. It is in our faith that we move ahead trusting in His word.

Looking at the Great Commission, there is still so much left to be done. It is worth it to continue this journey of faith and give our all to reach those who are less fortunate. Let us continue on this journey with your help and prayers and saying with heartfelt gratitude .... THANK YOU !!!!

CHARACTER

Bobby Jones was one of the greatest golfers to ever tee up a golf ball. Jones captured the "Grand Slam" of golf winning all four major tournaments in the U.S. and Britain in a single year. There are many accolades and achievements on his resume but I like most the story of him when after reaching the final playoff in the U.S. Open, he struck his ball in the rough while setting up for a shot. His iron accidentally touched the ball. He immediately notified the marshals and called a penalty on himself.

Since the marshals had not witnessed the ball strike, they left the decision to Jones, whether to invoke the two-stroke penalty. Jones called the penalty on himself, not knowing that he would lose the tournament by a single stroke. When praised for his honesty, he replied, "You may as well praise a man for not robbing a bank!" Jones may have lost the tournament, but his character was legendary and today the United States Golf Association's award for sportsmanship is known as the "Bobby Jones Award."

We have all heard many times that "Character is what you do when nobody is watching". Character is how you treat people who can do absolutely nothing for you. Character is how you react when the pressure is on in the dark. Character is being committed to doing the right thing regardless.

Practically every moment we have the opportunity to exercise character in our lives. Every day we're faced with decisions we make when no one is watching. It is our character that prompts us to do the right thing. We may not reap the dividends immediately but we are assured that God is keeping track of our decisions, and He will make good on every one!

Character cannot be developed in ease and quiet. Only through experience of trial and suffering can the soul be strengthened, ambition inspired and success achieved.
Helen Keller

FOCUS ON THE BIG PICTURE

I don't think you will get too much pushback from fellow golfers when declaring the golf swing is the most focused on element of the game. It lasts only a few seconds but think how important those few seconds are. The swing determines the distance and direction of the ball.

Any player who has ever taken lessons knows how coaches attempt to break down your swing. Factors such as ball height, grip, grip pressure, club selection, club angle, stance and much more all factors in the final product that flies off the club head after the swing. It's easy to obsess about one aspect of your swing and work incessantly on it. Where we many times fail is in not seeing the bigger picture and how that aspect fits into the overall swing performance.

Our lives can be like that. We can become so focused on our current circumstances that we lose perspective of the big, long term picture. Life can move us in compartmental spaces where we can sometimes feel trapped and hopeless. Many times we blame others for this "funk" and sometimes we even blame God.

What we must develop when mired in the funk is a change of perspective. Stop looking at the parts of our lives and see them in the context of the whole. If our lives are connected to Jesus, we regain the hope in knowing He is the One who holds each of us in the palm of His hand. There's hope in knowing the challenges we face have meaning, and lead to His revealing purpose in our lives.

Only in hindsight do we see the end result of the segment of life we are dealing with now, but Jesus not only knows in advance, He is holding it together for you and directing it toward His intended goal. Trust in His perspective and not yours.

NO ROLL THE DICE

Have you ever teed up on a hole with a sharp dog leg? You stand on the tee and have no visual contact with the flag. There may be potential hazards awaiting you that are not visible. The fairway is narrow and lined with sand traps and deep rough on either side. You do some mental distance calculation and conclude that you could possibly cut over the pond and rough on the left thus cutting the distance to the cup.

There's nothing like "going for it". If I can punch it between those two trees, I'm sure to turn a par 5 into a par 4 by cutting the corner! Every golfer knows the situation I'm describing. The temptation of a risky "roll the dice" shot has become each of us. Maybe you get lucky flying over the rough and water and somehow land in the fairway with a short approach chip to the green.

More times than not, I usually regret such foolishness. The smart golfer plays the fairway. Likewise, Jesus' words are pretty clear and simple when it comes to taking the wisest path foward in our life with God. If Jesus were a golfer, He just might suggest:

> "PLAY THE FAIRWAY. MANY PEOPLE TRY TO FIND SHORTCUTS AND ULTIMATELY END UP OUT OF BOUNDS OR IN THE DRINK. THE BEST WAY TO THE GREEN IS THE NARROW FAIRWAY, WHICH IS TOUGHER TO HIT AND THEREFORE FEWER TAKE IT."

SHOW ME THE SIGN

One beneficial feature of a golf course in the sign placed at the tee box of every hole. These signs contain valuable information for the golfer including pin placement, bunker locations and yardage info.

Got me to thinking ..... where would I be, where would I be headed without the marker lines represented by Jesus in my life. The short answer to that is "in the trap." The demons and temptations in today's society are well hidden. Pride, envy, jealousy and lust are just a few of the serpents that lie hidden under the rocks of this world ready to strike. The battle between good and evil within every Jesus follower is real. Check out Romans 7:14-25 for Paul's take on that. Conflict between our sinful nature and what Jesus wants us to be is played out constantly in our relationships at home, work and yes ...... among fellow believers.

What a friend we have in Jesus (good lyric for a song) as the marker lines in our life. His spirit and influence is there reminding us, encouraging us, loving and forgiving us as we navigate the winding, rolling and twisting fairways of life. We all travel the same road. We all face the extreme road conditions created by the storms in our lives. Brokenness, loss and defeat constantly blur our vision and tempt to derail our travel. God is our ball marker. He is our beacon, our GPS. He is our rest stop. It is in him that we find our destination. It is within His lines of holiness that we navigate through and around the reality of our own ungodliness. Pay attention to the signs - safe travels.

DIMPLES AND ALL

Gotta share this one with you by way of Phil Callaway. There are approximately 400 dimples in a golf ball. If you remove those dimples, the ball would only travel 60 to 80 yards when struck by the club. As surely as a golf ball needs these indentations, the trials (dimples) in our lives deepen us and put our character to the test. Difficult times can bring out the worst in us, but when we choose joy, embrace courage, and follow Jesus, they can help us discover the very best God has for us.

We all love mountaintop experiences, but we don't grow there. Life's larger lessons are learned most often through tough times. The trials of life also prepare us to help those who are experiencing difficulty. Second Corinthians 1:4 teaches that God comforts us in all our troubles so that we can comfort others.

Blessed be the God who consoles us in all our affliction, so that we may be able to console those who are in any affliction with the consolation with which we ourselves are consoled. ..... 2 Corinthians 1:4. If you are suffering - there is hope that at the end of the darkness - you will be stronger in your faith and better equipped to shine your light of God's love with the world.

__ADVICE FROM THE BEST__

"Success in this game depends less on strength of body than strength of mind and character."
Arnold Palmer

"A good golfer has the determination to win and the patience to wait for the breaks."
Gary Player

"As you walk down the fairway of life you must smell the roses, for you only get to play one round."
Ben Hogan

"Everybody can see that my swing is homegrown. That means everybody has a chance to do it."
Bubba Watson

"Resolve never to quit, never to give up, no matter what the situation"
Jack Nicklaus

"Discipline and concentration are a matter of being interested."
Tom Kite

"A routine is not a routine if you have to think about it."
Davis Love Jr.

CHECK YOUR CLUBFACE

All golfers know the key to hitting a good golf shot is striking the ball with the center of the club face. Strike the ball off center to the left or right and your ball travel will hook or slice. The folks who manufacture golf equipment spend millions trying to convince golfers that their product can "guarantee" the preferred shot.

Truth is, the straight shot is literally "in our own hands". If we properly address the ball with a nice even swing and strike the ball in the center of the clubface, good results will follow. Good results will follow regardless of the technology behind the club we are hitting.

Sounds a lot like life doesn't it. If we have the proper demeanor, character, attitude and behavior with people, our relationships will be what is desired. If we lie, cheat, abuse and harm the ones we come in contact with, our lives will be akin to a hook or a slice. We will not find ourselves in the center of the fairway of life.

Sometimes as I am cleaning my clubs, I notice the ball marks on the face of the clubs. The imprint of the ball strike is evident especially on the larger faces of your driver. There are marks dead center and there are ones to the left and right.

Fact is the sweet spot location will vary depending on the club and it's design. Usually on a blade type club it will be more toward the heel while on a driver, wood or putter, maybe a little more towards center. Same goes with our own personalities. Some of us are gruff and tough on the outside and caring and compassionate on the inside.

What is important is we realize how our demeanor and attitudes (clubface strike) affect our relationships with others (direction of our shot). Not only is it important to ensure our ball strike is correct but also to have an understanding that many we know are still learning to hit the ball.

CACOON

One of the most enjoyable things about playing golf for me is being able to spend some time outdoors. Most golf courses are well kept manicured places of natural beauty. The vegetation, water and tree lined rough areas are perfect habitats for all sorts of wildlife. I have seen squirrels (even an albino), fox, beavers, raccoons, all sorts of birds and even several alligators. A golf course with a beautiful natural setting combined with a challenging layout is a calming, relaxing place to spend some time. Especially if you're hitting the ball well.

Recently I was playing with a friend on a beautiful day on a very lush course. While I was teeing up my ball I noticed him examining some activity in a nearby scrub. I walked over and discovered he had found the plant covered in caterpillars. He was concerned about the infestation and began knocking them off with his golf club. I quickly grabbed his hand and asked him: "Do you like butterflies?" He responded, "Of course I love butterflies".

I gave him a short lesson on how one day soon those caterpillars he was murdering would be butterflies. He must have slept through biology class as a youngster. Like the caterpillar making his metamorphosis into a beautiful butterfly, God has designed our transformation to take place. "If a man die, shall he live again? All the days of my appointed time will I wait, till my change come." (Job 14:14)

As people we are changing all the time. As followers of Jesus, we grow upward into our next level of spiritual formation. Akin to the butterfly, we push our way out of the cocoon breaking free from all the fear, insecurity, apprehension, and drama thrown at us by our worldly existence. "Therefore, since we are surrounded by such a great cloud of witnesses, let us throw off everything that hinders and the sin that so easily entangles, and let us run with perseverance the race marked out for us, ..." (Hebrews 12:1)

Like the butterfly breaking out of his cocoon, it is time to take flight. Everything comes to full maturity in its time. Look up! It is time to rejoice! Your change has come!

WATER YOUR PLANTS

You are teeing off on a par four. You hit a great shot right down the middle of the fairway landing 125 yards from the green. You follow up with a nine iron shot hitting the green and rolling within 2 feet of the cut. You all but have a birdie on the score card. All you got to do is tap in a 2 foot putt. You set up, take your swing and the ball rolls straight towards the cup stopping ½ inches from the hole. So close BUT no birdie.

My wife is notorious for buying plants for our yard, bringing them home, unloading them from her car and sitting them in the driveway or garage. After a few days, I remind her of her recent purchase and make a loving, caring, gracious, soft and kind suggestion that she plant her new flowers. After a couple more weeks have passed, I inquire (again gently and mindful) in regards to her desired location of aforementioned plants. After several weeks of broken promises and unfulfilled commitments, all negotiations break down and I (yes ..... me) plant the flowers. This practice has gone on for 25 years and I hope it will continue for another 25.

Several weeks back, she bought a couple of plants for our butterfly garden. She unloaded them and sat them outside the garage (see ... I told you). The exact location of the plants just happened to be about 24 inches from a water faucet (I call them spickets).

I passed them several times a day paying little attention thinking only about me having to plant them in a few weeks (after negotiations with the wife break down).

One day last week I noticed the plants were really suffering for water so I reached with a bucket just 24 inches away and saved their life. A Jesus moment overcame me. How many people, places and things suffer, even to the point of death, when life saving means and methods are only inches away. How many neighbors just across the fence are carrying burdens and losing bouts with pain and suffering? How many problems at your door step go unattended when you have the means and ability to solve?

It is so important that we not become so busy and isolated that we miss opportunities in our lives to make the life of another better. Sometimes the voice of our brothers blood does cry to us from the ground (Genesis 4:10). Are we listening?

MR NICE GUY

Alice Cooper was a major rock star in the seventies. Although I was a huge music fan, Alice was not one of my favorites. I think it was the snakes and stuff ..... all the theatrical props kinda overwhelmed the music. Mr. Cooper however did have a couple of hits that would have been on my ITunes playlist. *Schools Out* and *No More Mister Nice Guy* were both great tunes. In *No More Mister Nice Guy,* Alice sang about the reactions of his mother's church group to his stage performances. He was attempting to say that there were worse things he could be doing with his life and now "the gloves are off." Hopefully now to the church groups approval, Alice has parlayed his music into a subdued and successful career that includes acting, restaurants, golf and hosting his own radio show.

Yes I said Alice Cooper is a golfer. Sporting a 5.3 handicap, he is a force to be reckoned with on the links. Today he plays 36 holes a day teeing off with Tiger Woods and Vijay Singh just to drop a few names. He has also appeared in ads for many golf equipment brands including Callaway. He has four holes-in-one and three double eagles. No bad for a snake handling rock star. Now he's Alice the "nice" guy.

A friend shared a thought provoking piece with me last week about being nice. I know what you are thinking ...... they were not insisting that I was not nice. Instead, the slant of the article was the huge difference between being "nice" and being "kind." A few thoughts to consider from the article, along with some of my own, are based on the fact that as we mature and are forced to face the realities of a broken world .... being nice is not always the right choice. With the ever-growing emphasis on political correctness, being nice can prevent one form expressing political or theological opinions. Being nice can trap and constrain you. It can prevent you from speaking up about injustice. It can shut you up when your voice needs to be heard.

Brings me to a few of my own thoughts. The deeper I ponder, the more I realize the two words are in no way interchangeable. Niceness can be quiet. Kindness speaks up. Niceness can leave problems undiagnosed. Kindness can heal. Niceness sometimes compromises what is right to keep the peace. Kindness stands firm in what is right with humility, gentleness and grace to create and sustain the peace. Niceness holds back. Kindness intervenes. Niceness conforms. Kindness confirms. Niceness flows from the heart. Kindness is a product of both heart and mind.

We all love the hero. The one who steps forward and tackles the playground bully who is abusing the weaker children. We all admire those who take the unpopular stance on meaningful issues while we stand and watch in a "nice" way. The circumstances in our world today are calling us to muster the courage to be "kind." "Kind" to those who are not "nice" to us. Proverbs 11:17 says that: "A man who is kind benefits himself." The world is full to the brim with "nice" folks. It's now time to be "kind." And remember above all that sometimes niceness isn't very kind at all.

SLOW IT DOWN

Patience is an important attribute in the game of golf. Well thought out play is a much better assurance of a low score than that of hasty play. Taking the time to plan your shot, select your club and take a relaxed non hurried swing is a good strategy.

In our culture, patience is becoming less and less common. We're an instant gratification society. When things don't go according to our timetable or plans, we get frustrated and sometimes angry. Biblical patience is a much-needed virtue these days, and certainly a reflection of where we are in our faith journey.

One faith based author defines patience as "that calm and unruffled temper with which the good man bears the evils of life, whether they proceed from persons or things. It also manifests itself in a sweet submission to the providential appointments of God and fortitude in the presence of the duties and conflicts of life."

How do we develop godly patience? By looking to Jesus Christ, who exhibited great patience and kindness toward His disciples and who does the same with us today. Instead of giving us the punishment we deserve for our sins, He gives us forgiveness. Instead of condemnation, He gives us grace. His patience with us creates patience in us, which we should then demonstrate to others.

DON'T FORGET TO PUTT

There are three basic shots in golf. First you hit the ball from the tee followed by an approach shot from the fairway to the green and finally you putt. You have only one tee shot. Depending on your skill and length of the hole, your approach shot strokes can vary. The same for your putting. The number of strokes it takes to hole the ball once you're on the green depends on many factors. Length of shot, condition of green, the lie and line all play a role when putting.

When I first became serious about the game, putting was the part of my game I focused on the least. Heck, I've been playing putt putt golf all my life. My attention and emphasis was my tee and approach shots. In time, you become more comfortable with your driver, woods, irons and wedges. Smacking the ball 200 plus yards off the tee and hitting the approach shot on the green will come with enough practice and play time. As your proficiency getting on the green increases, the more you realize the importance of your putting skills. Bad putts add strokes the same as a slice off the tee into the rough.

As I thought about this, I couldn't help but draw a comparison to my spiritual formation. In the beginning I was focused on the tee and approach shots. My tee shot was finding a church and becoming a part of a faith community. This was followed by my approach shot as I became involved in church leadership, ministry and mission participation. Over time, these get you off the ground, up and running as you make the transformative turn towards a faith based lifestyle. All that stuff is well and good but .... how's your putting?

Once you are in church - what are you doing out of church? Are you living into all those bible verses you've memorized? Are you emulating Jesus? Do you love those who don't love you? Are you feeding the hungry and clothing the naked? Does your Sunday spirit carry over into Monday? Are you as filled with joy at the office water fountain as you are in Sunday school?

Develop a strong, long and straight tee shot. Work on getting your approach shot tight and focused. And with all of that, be sure to work on your putting.

ROAR LIKE A TIGER

There is absolutely no doubt that Tiger Woods has had the greatest impact on the game of golf than anyone who has ever played the game. Less than one year after turning pro, Tiger was ranked number one in the world. His number one ranking covered over 545 weeks. He has won the PGA Player of the Year a record eleven times.

The records and accomplishments of this golf pro could go on for pages. With all his success, he more than any player before him, presented himself as an athlete. Tiger's commitment to fitness and a physical exercise regiment set him apart from all the other players on tour. And the results certainly speak for themselves.

Tiger trained at the highest level of fitness despite playing a sport that can produce legitimate competitors like John Daly and Craig Stadler. Tiger's focus on fitness has set the standards for some of today's best players like Dustin Johnson and Rory McIlroy.

Being at our top mental and physical form better prepares us to live our lives in maximum service to others. When we feel good, we look good. When we look good, we act good. Wellness is a celebrated place to be. Our bodies are of value to God. First Corinthians 6:19-20 reminds us that our body is a temple of the Holy Spirit.

Part of being a good steward of the bodies God has given us is intentionally learning how to best use them. While our occupations might not require the physical demands of Tiger, we all have a divine responsibility to care for ourselves.

A balanced approach to exercise and health is what followers of Jesus should pursue. However, in that pursuit we must not lose sight of God. The reason we should care for our bodies is not to prolong our own lives or better perform worldly tasks but rather because we value and desire to steward God's gift of life to us.

BOOK ORDER INFORMATION

Additional copies of this book along with my other books ***Gray Matter, Gray Matter .... Second Helping, Gray Matter ..... Just Sayin*** and ***Gray Matter ...... Journey of a Disciple*** are available through amazon.com.
Go to www.amazon.com **– click on books and type Teed Off Charlie Gray in the search block.**

Other sources of purchase include Amazon Create Space and Ingram. You may also receive copies by sending your request to charliegray@nc.rr.com.

Made in the USA
Columbia, SC
02 November 2021